ALTO SAX
101 WORSHIP SONGS

Available for
FLUTE, CLARINET, ALTO SAX, TRUMPET, VIOLIN

ISBN 978-1-70512-276-1

Visit Hal Leonard Online at **www.halleonard.com**

Explore the entire family of Hal Leonard products and resources

World headquarters, contact:
Hal Leonard
7777 West Bluemound Road
Milwaukee, WI 53213
Email: info@halleonard.com

In Europe, contact:
Hal Leonard Europe Limited
1 Red Place
London, W1K 6PL
Email: info@halleonardeurope.com

In Australia, contact:
Hal Leonard Australia Pty. Ltd.
4 Lentara Court
Cheltenham, Victoria, 3192 Australia
Email: info@halleonard.com.au

CONTENTS

ABOVE ALL

ALTO SAX

Words and Music by PAUL BALOCHE
and LENNY LeBLANC

Worshipfully

AMAZING GRACE
(My Chains Are Gone)

ALTO SAX

Words by JOHN NEWTON
Traditional American Melody
Additional Words and Music by CHRIS TOMLIN
and LOUIE GIGLIO

ANOTHER IN THE FIRE

ALTO SAX

Words and Music by
CHRIS DAVENPORT

Worship Ballad

ANCIENT WORDS

ALTO SAX

Words and Music by
LYNN DeSHAZO

AT THE CROSS
(Love Ran Red)

ALTO SAX

Words and Music by MATT REDMAN,
JONAS MYRIN, CHRIS TOMLIN,
ED CASH and MATT ARMSTRONG

BATTLE BELONGS

ALTO SAX

Words and Music by PHIL WICKHAM
and BRIAN JOHNSON

Moderate Rock feel

BECAUSE HE LIVES, AMEN

ALTO SAX

Words and Music by WILLIAM J. GAITHER,
GLORIA GAITHER, DANIEL CARSON,
CHRIS TOMLIN, ED CASH,
MATT MAHER and JASON INGRAM

Moderately

AS THE DEER

Words and Music by
MARTIN NYSTROM

BLESSED BE YOUR NAME

ALTO SAX

Words and Music by MATT REDMAN
and BETH REDMAN

Rhythmically

BEFORE THE THRONE OF GOD ABOVE

Words and Music by VIKKI COOK
and CHARITIE BANCROFT

With reverence

THE BLESSING

ALTO SAX

Words and Music by KARI JOBE CARNES,
CODY CARNES, STEVEN FURTICK
and CHRIS BROWN

BREATHE

ALTO SAX

Words and Music by
MARIE BARNETT

BROKEN VESSELS
(Amazing Grace)

ALTO SAX

Words and Music by JOEL HOUSTON
and JONAS MYRIN

Moderately

(small note optional)

BUILD MY LIFE

ALTO SAX

Words and Music by MATT REDMAN,
PAT BARRETT, BRETT YOUNKER,
KARL MARTIN and KIRBY KAPLE

Moderately slow

BUILD YOUR KINGDOM HERE

ALTO SAX

Words and Music by
REND COLLECTIVE

Upbeat Folk feel

COME, NOW IS THE TIME TO WORSHIP

ALTO SAX

Words and Music by
BRIAN DOERKSEN

CHRIST OUR HOPE IN LIFE AND DEATH

ALTO SAX

Words and Music by KEITH GETTY
MATT BOSWELL, JORDAN KAUFLIN
MATTHEW MERKER and MATT PAPA

GLORIFY THY NAME

Words and Music by
DONNA W. ADKINS

COME THOU FOUNT, COME THOU KING

ALTO SAX

Traditional
Additional Words and Music by
THOMAS MILLER

CORNERSTONE

ALTO SAX

Words and Music by JONAS MYRIN,
REUBEN MORGAN, ERIC LILJERO
and EDWARD MOTE

DAYS OF ELIJAH

ALTO SAX

Words and Music by
ROBIN MARK

GREAT IS THE LORD

Words and Music by MICHAEL W. SMITH
and DEBORAH D. SMITH

DO IT AGAIN

ALTO SAX

Words and Music by MATT REDMAN,
STEVEN FURTICK, CHRIS BROWN
and MACK BROCK

HOW DEEP THE FATHER'S LOVE FOR US

**Words and Music by
STUART TOWNEND**

Quietly

DRAW ME CLOSE

ALTO SAX

Words and Music by
KELLY CARPENTER

EVERLASTING GOD

ALTO SAX

Words and Music by BRENTON BROWN
and KEN RILEY

Moderate Rock

FOREVER

ALTO SAX

Words and Music by
CHRIS TOMLIN

FOREVER REIGN

ALTO SAX

Words and Music by JASON INGRAM
and REUBEN MORGAN

GIVE THANKS

ALTO SAX

Words and Music by
HENRY SMITH

GOOD GRACE

ALTO SAX

Words and Music by
JOEL HOUSTON

Moderately slow

GLORIOUS DAY

ALTO SAX

Words and Music by SEAN CURRAN
KRISTIAN STANFILL, JASON INGRAM
and JONATHAN SMITH

With energy

GOOD GOOD FATHER

ALTO SAX

Words and Music by PAT BARRETT
and ANTHONY BROWN

GOODNESS OF GOD

ALTO SAX

Words and Music by BEN FIELDING,
ED CASH, JASON INGRAM,
JENN JOHNSON and BRIAN JOHNSON

GRAVES INTO GARDENS

ALTO SAX

Words and Music by CHRIS BROWN,
STEVEN FURTICK, TIFFANY HAMMER
and BRANDON LAKE

GREAT I AM

ALTO SAX

Words and Music by
JARED ANDERSON

GREAT THINGS

ALTO SAX

Words and Music by JONAS MYRIN
and PHIL WICKHAM

Moderate Rock beat

GREAT ARE YOU LORD

ALTO SAX

Words and Music by JASON INGRAM
DAVID LEONARD and LESLIE JORDAN

Slowly, in 2

THE HEART OF WORSHIP
(When the Music Fades)

ALTO SAX

Words and Music by
MATT REDMAN

Steady Ballad

HERE I AM TO WORSHIP
(Light of the World)

ALTO SAX

Words and Music by
TIM HUGHES

Moderately slow, steady

HIS MERCY IS MORE

ALTO SAX

Words and Music by MATT BOSWELL
and MATT PAPA

Slow Gospel feel

HOLY IS THE LORD

ALTO SAX

Words and Music by CHRIS TOMLIN
and LOUIE GIGLIO

HOSANNA
(Praise Is Rising)

ALTO SAX

Words and Music by PAUL BALOCHE
and BRENTON BROWN

Moderately fast

HOLY SPIRIT

ALTO SAX

Words and Music by KATIE TORWALT
and BRYAN TORWALT

HE IS EXALTED

Words and Music by
TWILA PARIS

Flowing, in 2

HOUSE OF THE LORD

ALTO SAX

Words and Music by PHIL WICKHAM
and JONATHAN SMITH

HOW GREAT IS OUR GOD

ALTO SAX

Words and Music by CHRIS TOMLIN,
JESSE REEVES and ED CASH

Moderately slow

I GIVE YOU MY HEART

ALTO SAX

Words and Music by
REUBEN MORGAN

I WILL RISE

ALTO SAX

Words and Music by CHRIS TOMLIN,
JESSE REEVES, LOUIE GIGLIO
and MATT MAHER

IN CHRIST ALONE

Words and Music by KEITH GETTY
and STUART TOWNEND

Moderately slow

INDESCRIBABLE

ALTO SAX

Words and Music by LAURA STORY
and JESSE REEVES

With motion, in 2

LORD, I NEED YOU

ALTO SAX

Words and Music by JESSE REEVES,
KRISTIAN STANFILL, MATT MAHER,
CHRISTY NOCKELS and DANIEL CARSON

IS HE WORTHY?

ALTO SAX

Words and Music by ANDREW PETERSON
and BEN SHIVE

JESUS MESSIAH

ALTO SAX

Words and Music by CHRIS TOMLIN,
JESSE REEVES, DANIEL CARSON
and ED CASH

KING OF KINGS

ALTO SAX

Words and Music by SCOTT LIGERTWOOD
BROOKE LIGERTWOOD and JASON INGRAM

Moderately

KING OF MY HEART

ALTO SAX

Words and Music by JOHN MARK McMILLAN
and SARAH McMILLAN

Moderately slow

LAMB OF GOD

Words and Music by
TWILA PARIS

With emotion

THE LION AND THE LAMB

ALTO SAX

Words and Music by BRENTON BROWN,
BRIAN JOHNSON and LEELAND MOORING

LIVING HOPE

ALTO SAX

Words and Music by PHIL WICKHAM
and BRIAN JOHNSON

Moderately, with praise

MORE PRECIOUS THAN SILVER

Words and Music by
LYNN DeSHAZO

MAJESTY

ALTO SAX

Words and Music by
JACK HAYFORD

MIGHTY TO SAVE

ALTO SAX

Words and Music by BEN FIELDING
and REUBEN MORGAN

NO LONGER SLAVES

ALTO SAX

Words and Music by JONATHAN DAVID HELSER,
BRIAN JOHNSON and JOEL CASE

NOTHING ELSE

ALTO SAX

Words and Music by CODY CARNES,
HANK BENTLEY and JESSIE EARLY

O COME TO THE ALTAR

ALTO SAX

Words and Music by CHRIS BROWN
MACK BROCK, STEVEN FURTICK
and WADE JOYE

O CHURCH ARISE

ALTO SAX

Words and Music by KEITH GETTY
and STUART TOWNEND

O PRAISE THE NAME
(Anástasis)

ALTO SAX

Words and Music by MARTY SAMPSON,
BENJAMIN HASTINGS and DEAN USSHER

OCEANS
(Where Feet May Fail)

ALTO SAX

Words and Music by JOEL HOUSTON,
MATT CROCKER and SALOMON LIGHTHELM

LORD, I LIFT YOUR NAME ON HIGH

Words and Music by
RICK FOUNDS

ONLY KING FOREVER

ALTO SAX

Words and Music by MACK BROCK,
CHRISTOPHER BROWN, STEVEN FURTICK
and WADE JOYE

Joyfully, with a driving beat

ONE THING REMAINS
(Your Love Never Fails)

ALTO SAX

Words and Music by JEREMY RIDDLE,
BRIAN JOHNSON and CHRISTA BLACK

OPEN THE EYES OF MY HEART

ALTO SAX

Words and Music by
PAUL BALOCHE

Moderately fast

OPEN UP THE HEAVENS

ALTO SAX

Words and Music by JASON INGRAM,
STUART GARRARD, ANDI ROZIER,
JAMES MACDONALD and MEREDITH ANDREWS

SHINE, JESUS, SHINE

ALTO SAX

Words and Music by
GRAHAM KENDRICK

OUR GOD

ALTO SAX

Words and Music by JONAS MYRIN,
JESSE REEVES, CHRIS TOMLIN
and MATT REDMAN

THE POWER OF THE CROSS
(Oh to See the Dawn)

Words and Music by STUART TOWNEND
and KEITH GETTY

Moderately slow

RAISE A HALLELUJAH

ALTO SAX

Words and Music by JONATHAN DAVID HELSER,
MELISSA HELSER, MOLLY SKAGGS
and JAKE STEVENS

Moderate Rock beat

RECKLESS LOVE

ALTO SAX

Words and Music by CALEB CULVER
CORY ASBURY and RAN JACKSON

Slowly, in 2

RESURRECTING

ALTO SAX

Words and Music by CHRIS BROWN
MACK BROCK, STEVEN FURTICK
WADE JOYE and MATTHEWS THABO NTELE

REVELATION SONG

ALTO SAX

Words and Music by
JENNIE LEE RIDDLE

With praise

To Coda

D.S. al Coda

SHINE ON US

Words and Music by MICHAEL W. SMITH
and DEBBIE SMITH

RUN TO THE FATHER

ALTO SAX

Words and Music by RAN JACKSON,
MATT MAHER and CODY CARNES

SEE A VICTORY

ALTO SAX

Words and Music by CHRIS BROWN,
STEVEN FURTICK, JASON INGRAM
AND BEN FIELDING

SHOUT TO THE LORD

ALTO SAX

Words and Music by
DARLENE ZSCHECH

SPEAK O LORD

ALTO SAX

Words and Music by STUART TOWNEND
and KEITH GETTY

Prayerfully

STEP BY STEP

Words and Music by
DAVID STRASSER "BEAKER"

Moderately fast

THIS I BELIEVE
(The Creed)

ALTO SAX

Words and Music by BEN FIELDING
and MATT CROCKER

THERE IS A REDEEMER

Words and Music by
MELODY GREEN

Moderately

THIS IS AMAZING GRACE

ALTO SAX

Words and Music by PHIL WICKHAM,
JOSHUA NEIL FARRO and JEREMY RIDDLE

10,000 REASONS
(Bless the Lord)

ALTO SAX

Words and Music by JONAS MYRIN
and MATT REDMAN

Moderate Ballad

WHOM SHALL I FEAR
(God of Angel Armies)

ALTO SAX

Words and Music by CHRIS TOMLIN,
ED CASH and SCOTT CASH

WAY MAKER

ALTO SAX

Words and Music by
OSINACHI KALU OKORO EGBU

Moderately

WHAT A BEAUTIFUL NAME

ALTO SAX

Words and Music by BEN FIELDING
and BROOKE LIGERTWOOD

WHO YOU SAY I AM

ALTO SAX

Words and Music by REUBEN MORGAN
and BEN FIELDING

WORTHY IS THE LAMB

ALTO SAX

Words and Music by
DARLENE ZSCHECH

YES I WILL

ALTO SAX

Words and Music by MIA FIELDES,
EDDIE HOAGLAND and JONATHAN SMITH

WE FALL DOWN

ALTO SAX

Words and Music by
CHRIS TOMLIN

YOU ARE MY ALL IN ALL

By DENNIS JERNIGAN

YET NOT I BUT THROUGH CHRIST IN ME

ALTO SAX

Words and Music by MICHAEL FARREN,
JONNY ROBINSON and RICH THOMPSON

Worship Ballad

YOU ARE MY KING
(Amazing Love)

ALTO SAX

Words and Music by
BILLY JAMES FOOTE

YOUR GRACE IS ENOUGH

ALTO SAX

Words and Music by
MATT MAHER

YOUR NAME

ALTO SAX

Words and Music by PAUL BALOCHE
and GLENN PACKIAM